a beginning!

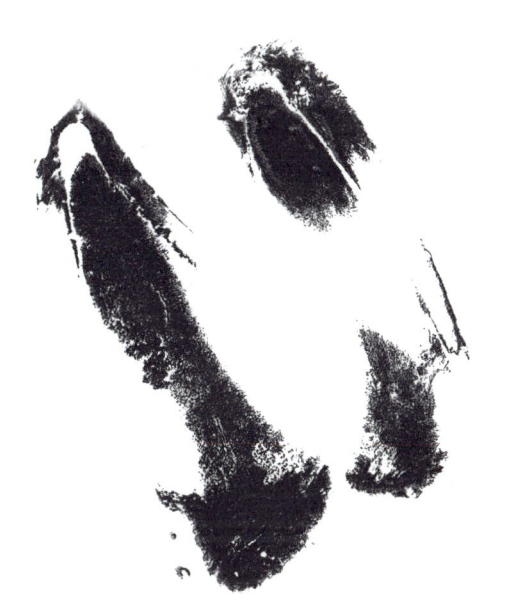

WIESINGER
PRINT | AUDIO | VISUAL

FIRST PRINT EDITION
Copyright © 2022 CHELSEY WIESINGER
All rights reserved.

LIBRARY AND ARCHIVES CANADA DATA
ISBN: 978-1-7386505-0-7

Publisher: WIESINGER Books
Cover Design: Romeo Finn
Illustrations: Romeo Finn

Without limiting the rights under copyright reserved above, no part of this publication may be reproduced, stored in or introduced into a retrieval system, or transmitted, in any form or by any means (electronic, mechanical, photocopying, recording or otherwise), without the prior written permission of both the copyright owner and the above publisher of this book.

The scanning, uploading, and distribution of this book via the Internet or via any other means without permission of the publisher is illegal and punishable by law. Please purchase only authorized electronic editions and do not participate in or encourage electronic piracy of copyright materials. Your support of the author's rights is appreciated.

caramel popc
peach
rainbow ribbon
bubble gum
goat berries (poop)
berry
sour patch kid
sucker
sour key
gummy worm
gummy bear
s'mores kit
runts
cola bottle
COLA
chocolate malt balls
razzles
goodies
bubble tap

chocolate bar
sweedish fish
smarties
pixie stix
taffy
liquorice rope
jelly beans
fuzzy peach
marshmallow banana
cotton candy
peanut butter cup
rainbow marshmallow
nerds
sour key
frog
gummy bear
rainbow lolly
liquorice
marshmallow strawberry
nibs

For the children, childlike,
and [goat] kids.
Also, for Ivan and Tonto.

An UnforGOATable True Story

BY CHELSEY WIESINGER

ILLUSTRATIONS BY ROMEO FINN

Ivan is a goat.
A mix of Saanan and Alpine
(which <u>might</u> be why he is so big).

When people say "The Goat,"
it means the

Greatest
Of
All
Time

WINK

Ivan's candy name is Marshmallow. He is

white

black

and golden

like a perfectly roasted marshmallow.

But you may ask: "Why would a goat have a candy name?"

Well, it's part of his unforgoatable story:

Once upon a time, in a summer village on a lake, my family laid our very old dog to rest,
and was very sad.

We weren't ready for a new dog.

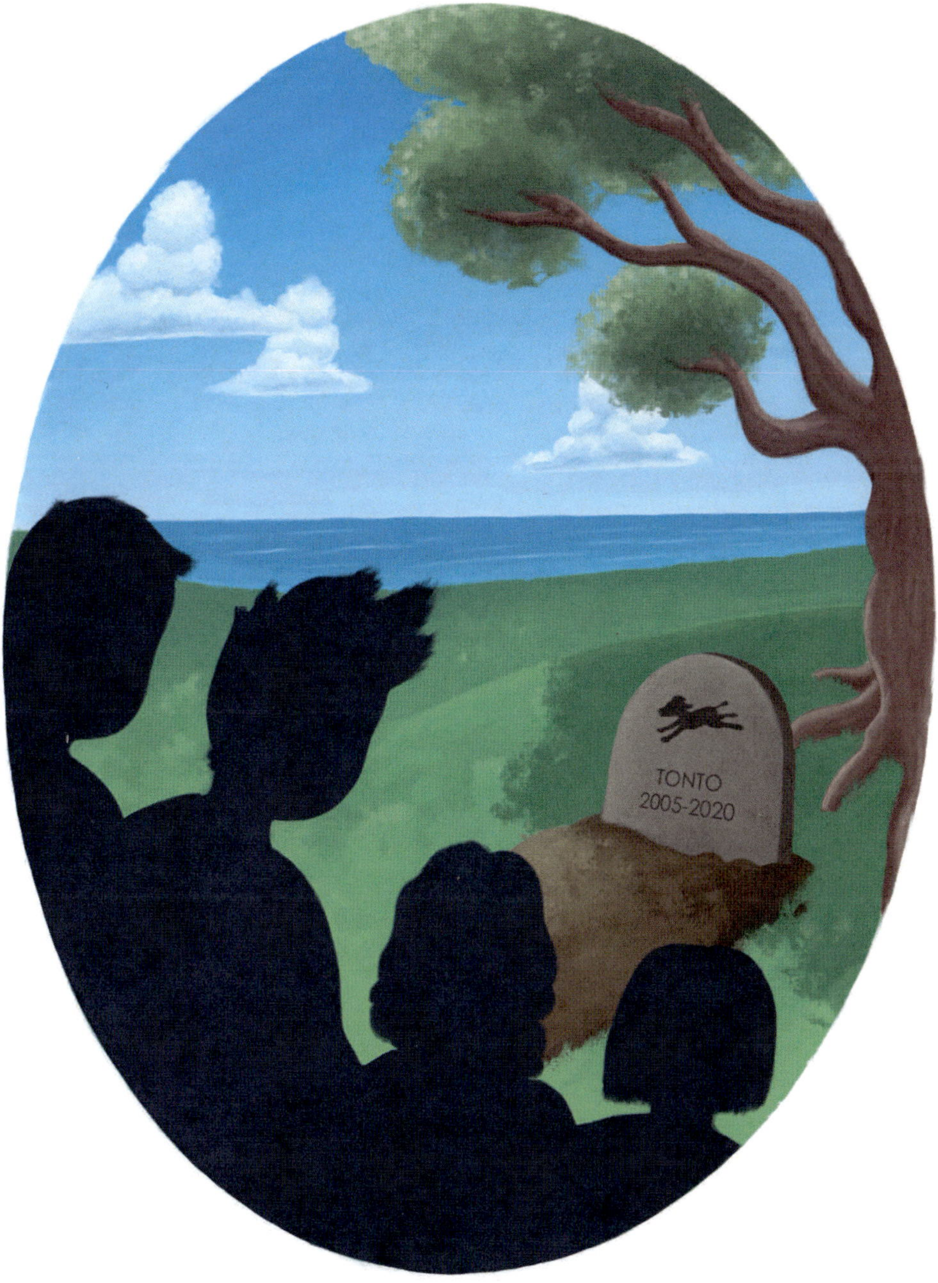
TONTO
2005-2020

So we did some research and thought about the future.

Alpaca's were too big.
And spit. A lot.

Piglets didn't stay small (or cute)!

Poof

Bernese mountain dogs
were too hairy.

Dad said: "Let's go on a trip."

Mom said: "Maybe something will come across our path."

Sure enough, it did.

While we were camping at a weekend family fun event, someone drove by on a goat cart.

YES!
A goat was pulling a person on a cart!

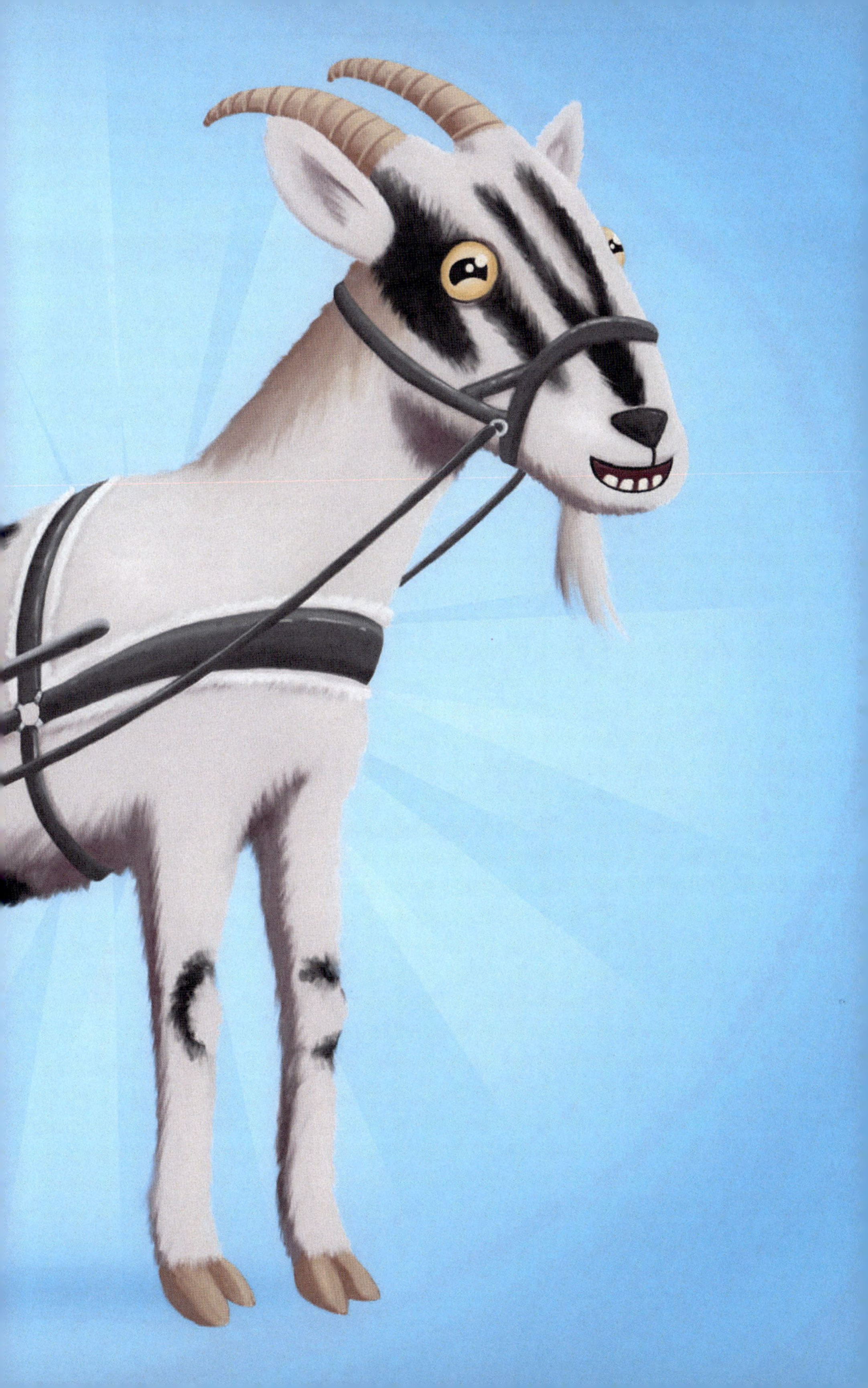

Mom looked at dad and said: "He could lead a parade in our summer village, like your hero Bob Goff."

Dad looked at mom and said: "He could pull a candy cart, like you did when you were a kid."

*Ivan is the 8th goat that Julia trained to pull cart. She is one of nine children of a musical family who live on a self-sustaining farm in Northern Alberta. Julia said "Ivan is the sweetest, kindest, and most affectionate goat she has trained!"

We made a family decision to adopt Ivan, with us kids even committing part of our weekly allowance for his care and keeping.

Some good friends helped us get ready for Ivan. We:

Put up a strong fence.

Built a comfy shed.

Added fun things to climb on.

And of course, had lots of things to eat.

It turns out Ivan doesn't like grass much

    (except the long, green grass which grows at the edge of the lake and has never been stepped on).

His main diet is hay and alfalfa, but...

Raspberry

Birch

Fireweed

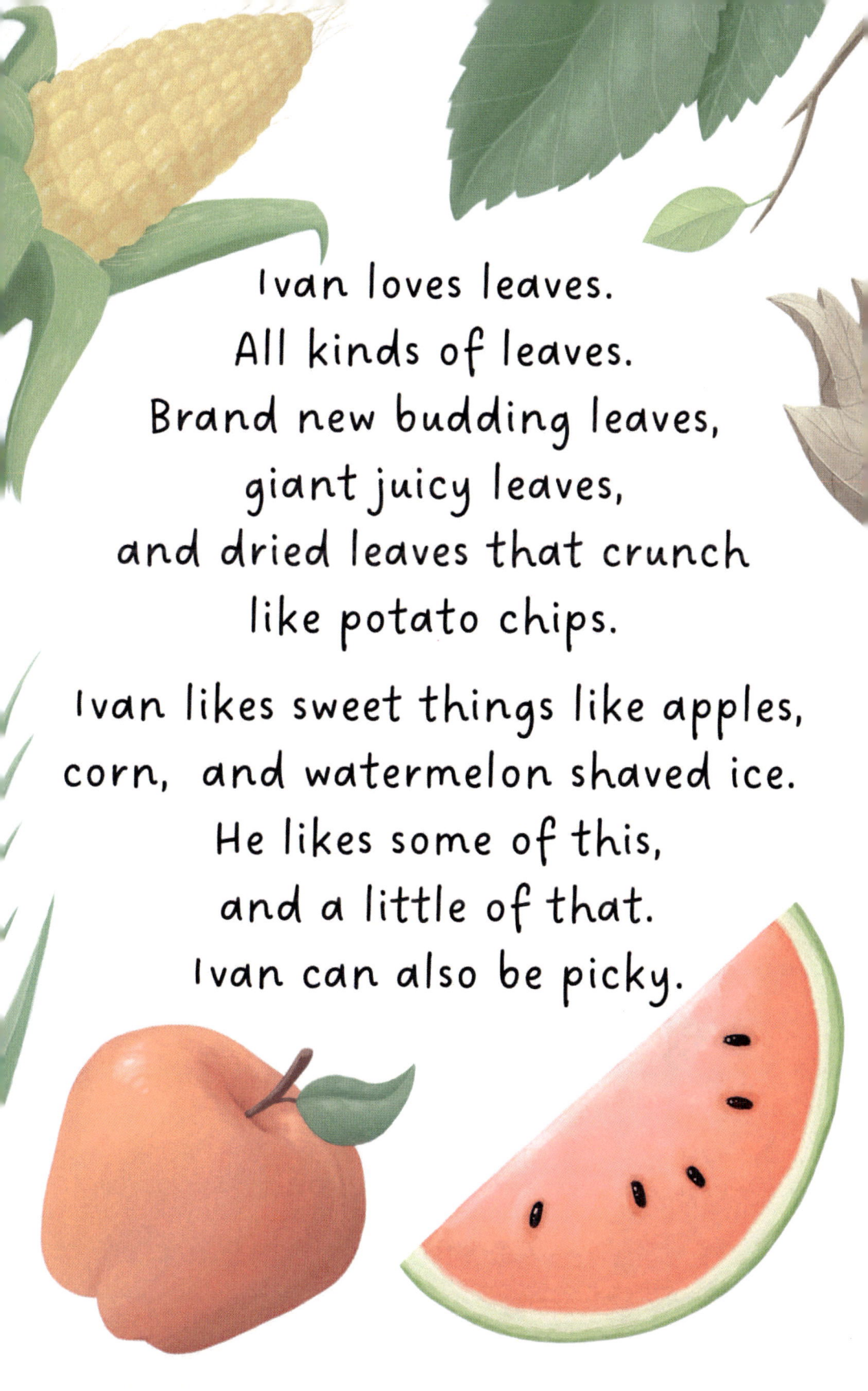

Ivan loves leaves.
All kinds of leaves.
Brand new budding leaves,
giant juicy leaves,
and dried leaves that crunch
like potato chips.

Ivan likes sweet things like apples,
corn, and watermelon shaved ice.
He likes some of this,
and a little of that.
Ivan can also be picky.

But there was more for Ivan to do than stand around and eat.

Papa helped us build a special cart out of our old stroller.

We bought lots of candy and treats to fill the cart.

Ivan pulled the candy cart around our summer village. We played music like an ice cream truck to draw attention.

On our first day we sold quite a bit, and Ivan got lots of smiles and scratches and leaves.
Everyone had fun!

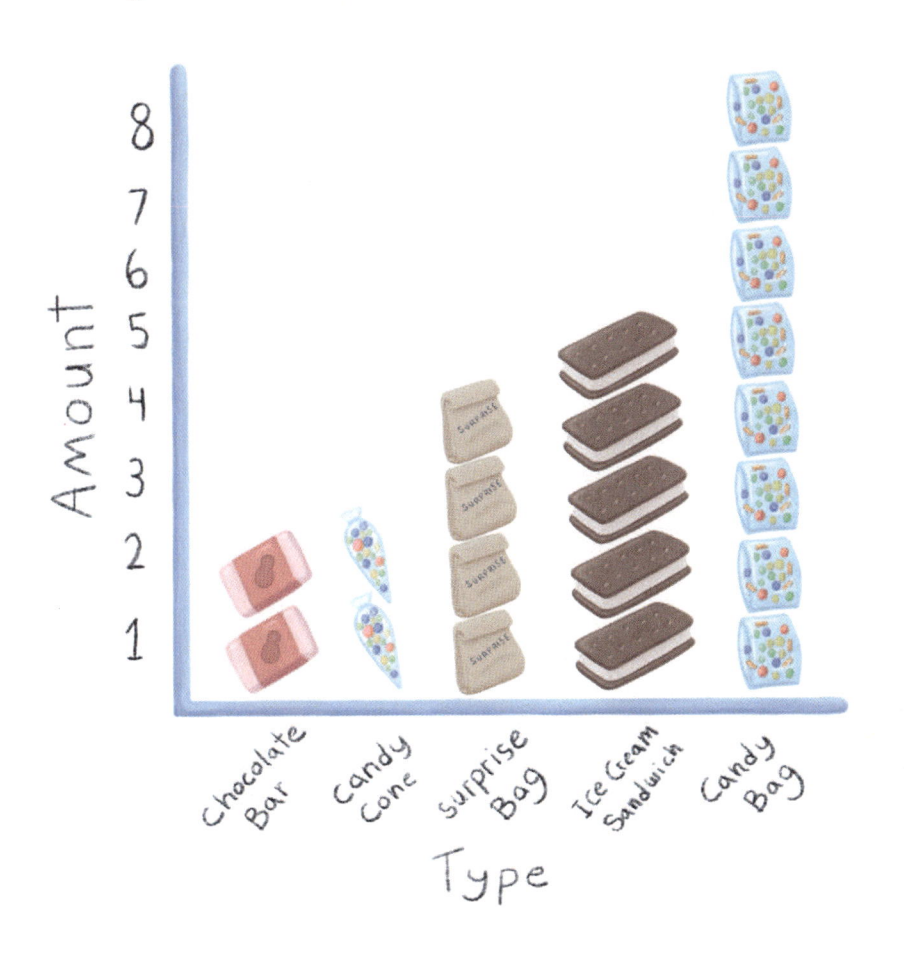

We were getting to know our neighbours and learning how to run a business
(not eating the profits is just one part!).

People started talking about Unforgoatable Treats.

Before long,
Ivan was invited to special events.

Ivan went to a cowboy ranch market.

He finished some watermelon shaved ice for those who couldn't do it on their own.

He posed in selfies.

Ivan went to a summer solstice metaphysical and artisan market.

A witch gave him a hug.

A depressed teenager who had never seen or touched a real, live goat before found wonder and cried tears of joy.

The police showed up.

One of the officer's asked: "Would Ivan be the ring bearer at my wedding?"

Ivan went to a summer camp.

200 kids crowded around and bought ALL his candy. Some nice volunteers stepped up to help out.

Ivan stood patiently and got more pats and scratches than ever before.

Sometimes the days were hot and long.
But Ivan had a job to do.

This included breaks to help keep him feeling good and on his best behaviour.

Ivan went to a big city church. He went into the building and walked across the big new stage.

Ivan was a little wide-eyed and nervous, but everyone cheered and rushed outside to meet him.

A young lady there asked: "Would Ivan work with seniors?"

Ivan went to visit grandmas and grandpas at four seniors' lodges around the big city.

"That's a big goat!" They said. Some even remembered having goats when they were a kid.

They took pictures and had something new and exciting to talk about,

and a little something sweet to share and enjoy.

All too soon the leaves began to change colour, and Ivan was let loose to munch them up before the snow came.

Candy carting was done for a season.

People can hardly believe their eyes
- and can't help but smile -
when they see Ivan pulling
his candy cart.

Ivan serves others
and brings joy wherever he goes.

That's why he's unforGOATable.

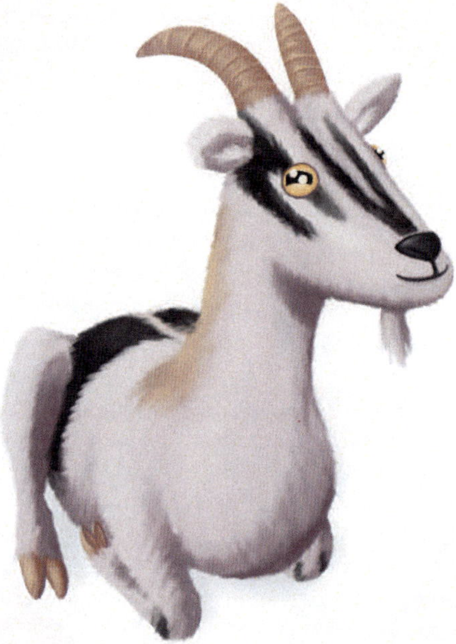

And his story is just a beginning.

caramel popc
peach
rainbow ribbon
bubble gum
goat berries (poop)
berry
sour patch kid
sucker
sour key
gummy worm
gummy bear
s'mores kit
runts
cola bottle
COLA
chocolate malt balls
goodies
razzles
bubble tap

I really did pull a candy cart when I was a kid (thanks mom & dad for sparking my entreprenurial spirit). The rest of this story is true too, though we are still waiting to see Ivan blow a bubble after all his chewing!

~ Chelsey

Ivan on the internet

https://zez.am/UnforgoatableTreats

Manufactured by Amazon.ca
Bolton, ON